Little Mirror

Little Mirror

poems

David Weiss

LynxHousePress
Spokane, Washington

Cover design: Joshua Unikel
Cover photo: Mauricio Navarrete Contreras
Author photo: Eric Bulson

FIRST EDITION

Cataloging-in-Publication Data is available from the Library of Congress.

ISBN 978-89924-182-1

To those steadfast ghosts
only the mirror can see

Contents

Every child, as he wakes into life,
finds a mirror underneath his pillow.
                    — W. H. Auden

A mirror broken in two is two mirrors

. . . a wilderness of mirrors.
                    — T. S. Eliot

came to
a mirror shop
what a jolt —
I could've been
some bum walking by
                    — Ishikawa Takuboku

Let's see you find the world now
                    — Vasko Popa

1

Inside the little mirror you wouldn't suspect
there's a slow mudslide of clear liquid

like the dead cities
of Herculaneum and Pompeii

where the temples and houses
of Isis   of the Deer   of the Black Room

lie buried   preserved
Put your eye to the edge

of the little mirror
and you'll see a prismatic effect

that will set you dreaming —
the only excavation possible

There's the smallest breeze   and a fox
moving through the orchard

There are the lone lights
of a car

and a possum crossing the road
There's a child sweating in her sheets

and a lamp shining down
on a cold cup of tea

A fog crawls up the river
and a beacon flashes its warning

Morning is still hours away
the floor underfoot cold

Whatever was said is still being said
Whatever was done is having

its repercussions
A cloud puts its hand over the moon's mouth

The little mirror never sleeps
keeping vigil

The little mirror is
neither digital nor analog

No password or power supply
is required

It will neither record nor retain data
but can be relied on

to keep all your secrets
without the least encryption

Set it on the floor   you're airborne
Hold it overhead   it's your coffin

Step back and there's enough room in it
to hold all of us   a happening   a mass grave

No message will come back from its depthless depths
No witness

No crime can be prosecuted with its help
If the little mirror has a shortcoming

it's this —
it will keep mum

even about a child
one of the world builders

playing dress up
in front of it

4

Only in song do you get there
only through the minor fall

Only in mind
For as long as the chord lasts

In the wide wide world
there are no scales

There   noise takes its rightful place
It's beautiful   and like music

compels assent
as these stiffened reeds scratching the windowpane

do
compelled themselves

by something
that's also irresistible

5

The little mirror
keeps a bible in its back pocket

When it comes across someone in need
it tears out a page

folds it into a little mirror
and hands it to him

whose eyes are watering
from hacking up a thick gob of green phlegm

He'll wipe his mouth with it
and drop it on the sidewalk

a scented remembrancer

6

Snow is coming down
again   little mirror

I can see it in your eye
On the long tongue

of fly paper
in front of the window

a wasp is stuck to it by a single wing
plus a stink bug and five unbuzzing flies

the recent historical record
Through the snow

a lattice of vines
snarls the hackberry tree

and beyond the uncombined corn field
a hedge row of winter trees

which shaded the field in summer
Little mirror

I once shaved under your jagged gaze
in a hurry

to look presentable
to look as if I belonged

No longer in a rush
you and I are left

to our own devices
to register without drama

what it feels like to be
here   now

deaccessioned

7

The little mirror
is a portal that even the molten sky

of morning
must pass through

Look down:
the ground below your feet is impenetrable

Nematodes and heavy equipment
move through it

far below the surface
Look up:

the cosmos isn't
anything you imagine it to be

At the bottom of the well
or beyond the furthest star

the little mirror
with its mind of matter

feels right at home

8

If you were a one-way mirror
think how simple life would be:

See-through from one side
opaque from the other

Vulnerable on one side
scary on the other

Like squinting out through a filthy windowpane
versus wearing dark shades

To observe without being seen
to listen in without being discovered

one of the great dreams
That's the problem

thinks the little mirror
Everybody wants to be a god

There is a bird that can only be heard by someone
who has come to be alone.

— Tony Hoagland

So many friends I have thought about
and not written to   or called
little mirror

so many children I have smiled at
to keep them from feeling
scared   or crying

so many dogs I have held my hand out to
palm up
to preempt their growling

so often grateful
to be like a trash bag on the side of the road
which no one stops to examine or pick up

The sad thing   little mirror
is I can live with that
a while longer

and yet I cannot listen
to the three notes of the mourning dove
without being felled by pity

each note an ax
taking a deeper bite until even a light breeze
can push me over

> *In the mirror, at night*
> *Strike the brief yellow flare of a match*
> *You'll glimpse the threat in the wound of dark*
> *that heals quickly — scarless*
> *— Ivan Lalić*

The match flares up before the little mirror
and there it is — not one but two burning tips

and behind them   a face I hope never to see again
that keeps looking with curiosity at this one

that dislikes the other intensely
as if that were in any way meaningful

Like   dislike: so petty
Young   old: so petty

Smart   stupid: so petty
good   bad: the same

The two flames   like holes in cambric
burn down   having gorged on the splinter of wood

Even in the dark now
I can make out the smoke twisting up

and I can smell it —
one thing becoming another

the universe revealing a trick
it's got up its sleeve:

there's never less than two of everything

11

Everything's spinning
little mirror   and I have fallen

flat on my back
even before I think to sit down

Geese are rowing overhead
bullied by a stiff gale

coming from who knows how far off . . .
Is anything not in motion

Earth whirls on its tether
turns on its axis

Above me wind lashes the branches
like a clutch of snakes touched by a cattle prod

The trouble with vertigo:
Is the world turning or has the center slipped its mooring

With you   little mirror
the angle of incidence

is equal to the angle of reflection
your one abiding belief

Unlike us   whatever enters you
emerges unchanged

12

No one can see themselves whole
little mirror

No one can hold in mind
all they are

No one can agree
We're each the stranger in our midst

A child frightened by a joyful dog
that jumps at her face

opens a hall of mirrors
convex and concave

You know all about that
little mirror

you show us how minuscule
the whole can actually be

how in the least of things
the rest is lurking

like a tulip petal
one so dark it's almost velvet

that loosens
then gives way

We feel it give
and our heart

— you can decide what that stands for —
goes out to it

13

Once   little mirror
I worked my brain to the bone

which isn't saying much
I was trying to set down

what had happened to me
and the part I played

I couldn't seem to do it
without embellishing

Soon I couldn't distinguish
what I made up

from what I thought took place
What I had her say was

so much more illuminating
than what she hadn't

Plus the heart of the matter
was obscure and elusive

and before long I was being
faithful

to what I had written
not to events

which I had not understood
the first time round

and she was long dead by then
Pity for my stupidities

drove me to make restitution
to actualities

I could not depict fairly —
some of which I could barely recall

In real life
there was no saving us

and what justice I could do
involved giving phantasy

and unlikely likelihoods their due
in constructing the fabric

of a carbolic realism
that felt true

I made up scenes
that took on a life of their own

which you   little mirror
would have known all about

looking   as you do   unflinchingly
at the dirty grout

of bathroom tiles that smell of
bleach and eyeliner

or the bright necklace in the fist
of a child tottering toward

her mother   or where she should have been
and was

no longer because
well   it hurts to think about

how soon the hurts begin
no getting back to scratch

though maybe back to 10^{-30} of the first second
is good enough

to keep going
to move in the direction

of making amends
and of making the painful

feel properly painful

14

Little mirror
Once you were part of something bigger than yourself

something a person could stand before
as if before a court of law   or his maker

and see himself
as he really was   at least in outline

before an instant of carelessness
or rage   or accident

changed everything
and you became what you are

a part of the shatter
that fell behind the dresser

to be overlooked
in the general sweeping up

That's how a career unexpectedly begins
how a life can acquire purpose

how contingency
will bless and bedevil us

— the right place at the wrong time
a demon in the mind

Anyone who has stared into
your unblinking uncomprehending eye

may see something essential
surrounding him- or her- or their selves

15

What I have learned from the little mirror:

to be passed by without so much as a glance

to whistle in the dark

to sense weightless motes in the air

that serendipity is a fraternal twin of misfortune

that your only thoughts are those reflected back to you

to know more about minutiae than you let on

the emptiness of time   the emptiness of space

about the quiet of perseverance

that nothing is incomplete

that everything is

that whoever comes through the door will be a stranger   more or less

to have no story of your own and still to enter it into the record

that others will turn away and still be visible to you

16

Little mirror
when you lie face up

on the ocean floor
among the gaudy sea cucumbers

the gloom at such great depth
will be absolute

To call you a mirror then
will be purely nominative

In that deep trench
etymology won't mean a thing

as it didn't to the man
on board ship

who found you in his coat pocket
and wondering why on earth

he brought it along
chucked you overboard

to tumble
into unending night

Flat on your back
you won't mind the pressure

or the dark
or the holothurians inching over you

That's the difference between us
I can't imagine those sea cucumbers —

photographs of them really —
without seeing them nubbed and spiny

parti-colored   cheery
as Christmas ornaments

Probabilities are all around
little mirror

like this cloud of gnats
about my head

They morph into turkey vultures
as they lift upward

to circle high overhead
like interlocking gold rings

Banking   they never once
bother

to flap their wings
Moving beneath spruce trees

I am   to them   just one
of the improbabilities

not worth much more
than a glance

The little mirror thinks about the largest mirror in the world
about how many little mirrors could fit inside it

and then whether all the mirrors in the world
could fit inside it at the same time

Would this mirror look like a school of fish or a flock of starlings
the whole not a whole at all   but only moving as one

That's what god would be like   the single mind of everything
the little mirror thinks   if the little mirror thought

That's what choreography   that's what
synchronized swimming want to be like

that's what thinking is
thinks the little mirror without any effort at thought

More evidence of how hard we must work to feel intact
Whereas I   thinks the little unthinking mirror   am so tuned in

that I flinch only and exactly when you flinch
Identity is perfect reflection   thinks the unreflective little mirror

On a clear night the immense salt flat of Uyuni is a looking glass
the cosmos holds up to observe itself

to see if it's beautiful and good and entire
terms unfamiliar and irrelevant to the little mirror

Even if you won't look at me
little mirror

I'll still look you in the eye
No judgment   no irony   no distaste

What you see is what I am
a boy

for one thing
who killed his great-grandfather

a leathery old man with a wooden cane
who lived like a troll

in the basement
who shook kosher salt

on buttered toast
for me

a fat little boy
with a long way to go

who'd never imagined
the Old Testament

rage
that could flare up

You can see the result
in the lines of my lips

pinched like a string purse
drawn shut

Terrified
I laughed as he thundered

at my clumsiness
and at my disobedience

He'd warned me not to
run over

his foot with my bike
Then he died

You can see it
little mirror   fear

in the form of dread
around the eyes

and wariness
that lightning can strike

out of the bluest of skies

Where love is concerned
little mirror

you know next to nothing
No sympathies slip in

to color your gaze
You're an equal opportunity noticer

One way or the other
it's all the same to you

When things don't work out
as planned

it's not your fault
You're like the old salt

fishing on the pier
who sits on his cooler

and smokes a pipe
as the line bobs

in the water all day
No expectations

he takes whatever comes
He won't let on

and you'd never guess it
that the only thing

he's interested in
is the one that got away

21

You're a footprint
little mirror   filling with water

an echo so faint
it's heard as an unvoiced thought

Early
you're positioned as the dearly departed

Late
you're the driver   behind the wheel of the hearse

You are prolific   if duplication is prolific
But no one will weep

or mind seeing the back of you
Until the doubts set in

no one needs you at all

This bone-white head of a doll
that lies beside the Titanic 12,000 feet down

is no bigger than you
little mirror

Bone-white with a greenish patina
of proteobacteria

halomonas titanicae at work
Soon the entire ship will be digested

by it
the salvaged artefacts already auctioned off

Tours of the wreck   it says
will commence in 2019

There will be little to see in ten years' time
But there'll still be song

old celluloid   underwater video
books   exact replicas

Shine   that invincible man
will still be swimming on

and he'll have the bald head in his pocket
eerie as a voodoo doll

because something always survives
to haunt the living

23

I don't remember my mother's young face
little mirror

but I can see her
holding up her hand mirror

turning her head   side to side
assessing

as far below I watched her
the bathroom steamy and warm

What does one do
with that

with the little happinesses
which have their home

in us
and nowhere else

in the known universe

24

What's the best we can hope for
little mirror

a front row seat
a leg up
a second chance
one hand washing the other
a joke we've never heard
an opening up in the chest
a month in the country
anything in the nick of time
the relief of giving up
nothing left to gain   nothing left to lose
no strings attached
a baby's hand clutching your finger
walking on air   walking on water
someone to turn and face you
an inside straight
a gannet flashing from the sky like a shooting star
a sense of absurdity   its bubble wrap
someone saying *it's okay*   in the most comforting way you can imagine

Little mirror
what would you know about any of this

25

Like a return of serve
you send back

facsimiles of what you see
with a bit of spin on each one —

a smudge   a scratch in your foil backing
some clouding

a reminder
that everything returned

adds a piece of itself to us
since we're made of

sleight of hand and apoptosis
miscalculation   forgetfulness

and on occasion
the grace of singing in tune

of pleasing someone
Some days   we feel like shit

others   inexplicably
we are buoyed up

we don't know by what
And when it's all over for us

kaput   we'll still be around
as stain or stitch or slow dispersal

or   like a yellowed beech leaf
found in the pages of a book

meaningful   for the trace of us
it seems to contain

though why we'd put it just there
is unclear

if it was even us that put it
there

Maybe the leaf   perfectly preserved
will be allowed to flutter to the floor

done with symbolism
and its wishful thinking

You're not much
little mirror
though you'll never get old

You'll never glimpse in the mirror
this stick figure
with a face now like a dried creek bed

If I put another mirror
right in front of you
you and it

will see only
an infinite regress of
emptiness

a tunnel moving off in both directions
that leads nowhere
But I can close my eyes

to see
I can close my eyes to hear something
ringing out

through the winter woods
not with song exactly
but with a force of inquiry

amplifying the silence
purifying the cold
and the bright white snow

Massive   pterodactylian
with a slash of feather red
on its head

a pileated woodpecker
its beak
driving in past bark

It sounds
a great   relentless
not until

For this
I'll use my paltry artifice

Little mirror
I shy from the major lift

however much I resonate
knowing

it will last only as long
as the lifting takes

before the hurt
has to be felt again

I get down on my knees
then   and feel for you in the icy mud

little mirror
who've fallen into it   face first

Feeling around   I'm stupid
as I've been all my life

lost
walking in circles

until the lift begins   unbidden
major   or not

emerging in the smallest detail
from the least seed

like the one now caught in my teeth
which cracks open

to release
a perfect bonsai of flavor

in this case
of a dried Calimyrna

fig

Little mirror
the going on we can't keep on doing

and do
is not a problem for you

What you're doing and go on doing
isn't much

You take what's given
A word like *strive* just makes you laugh

The words on this page are laughing
Me too

I think of Samuel Beckett
crossing a street in Paris

one shoelace undone
He stood on the corner

even after the light changed
unsure

whether to bend over
and tie it   or not

Night turns the mirror black

Standing before the little mirror
in the pitch dark

you stare   as if   at yourself
Those who see are cursed

by needing to be seen
A tiny mirror is tattooed

on our brain
It gives us all the comfort

that goes with
looking over our shoulder

and noticing
nothing out of the ordinary

and yet it's clear
that something using its tiny

mirror
has its eye on us

The Bald Eagle . . . is a Bird of bad moral Character
— Benjamin Franklin

The bald eagles nesting in the pine
have taken you for one of their own

They have looked you in your glassy eye
and seen what an apex predator looks like

rapt   observant   fear-free
opportunistic   single-minded

incurious   a scavenger
attracted to the dead

as well as the living
to take a synonym for *to kill*

They blink to wipe dust from their corneas
the better to see you   little mirror

the better to see you with
You'd never know it   listening

to their whingy high-pitched voices
that tuneless means: without remorse

Little mirror
how easy it would be to
cut you down

to size
You'd be restored to beach sand
plus some silver   some aluminum

which will blow away
as waves rolling in
pound the shore

while schools of small silvery fish
nose peaceably
beneath the kelpy surface

To think
how easy it would be . . .
is not to do it though —

Forget
how ridiculous it is
that I'm talking to you

To entertain an idea free
of consequence
is what makes thought

take wing
and allows for our double life —
the one we're living

in which possibilities wink out
like stars at dawn
extinguishing our wishes

and the one lived in mind
where anything goes — how
one person can use others

as if no one else were
of any importance
is understandable in

the experimental chambers of the mind
without it being any less loathsome
any less criminal

32

Little mirror
when I kneel on you

one knee at a time
I am always surprised you don't crack

any further than you already have
— my face in you made up of

five partial faces
poorly pieced together

as if from five different decades
— which is one approach to autobiography —

all the fault lines where one mistake has tried
to make up for another

Kindness no cure for absence
Affection no cure for a waning of eros

On time no fit response to *mistrust*
Moving on no fit response to *ordeal*

The pieces   mismatched
drift apart like continents

And in the widening space between
waters pour   salted and dark

Little mirror
I've broken objects other than you

things I've dropped
or kicked

or tightened
one too many turns

things I said
that couldn't be taken back

things I left out in the rain
to rot

things I ruined
that weren't things at all

that I could have salvaged
or mended or restored

but didn't
preferring the drag of failure

and blame
as if I had it coming

as if that would ensure
I would not forget who I really was

Little mirror
all you can remember to do

is show whoever gazes at you
face to face

what he looks like
at that very moment

All I can remember
is what comes to mind

unwilled
at any given moment

What I'm saying here
may be some kind of mentation

but it's not remembering
The old dog I lost for good

in a cemetery
whose back legs were so stiff

she walked as if on tiptoe
I *am*

recalling   pulling her up
hand over hand

from the well of forgetfulness
— likely because

for half an hour in the woods
this morning

I hollered for a dog
I'd lost

and now I am searching
for the one I never found

not in the pound
or among the headstones

on that cold autumn night
who died in a way

I rarely forget
that I'll never know

35

for SK

The unreal place between seasons
is where the work is done

If it had a mind to
a fly could observe its own abdomen

as it crawls over you
little mirror

Like anything without thought or volition
you're a keeper of the unreal place

we can't live without
returning to

It's like a green valley
locked away

by impenetrable mountains
as near   and as overlooked

as the hairs in your nose
which you have

only when I'm looking at you
head on

That's a going   and a coming back
we do

not as diplomats   but as smugglers

36

Little mirror
what would I do without you

to keep me honest
With you the scale is always

one-to-one
You're here to point out

that maps lie
Someone has to say

that proportion
is not the same as truth

someone has to stand up for
the microscope

and the teeming life
of metamorphic exchange

that doesn't meet the eye
and seethes like a jiggle of maggots

It's like 9 a.m. on a Saturday morning
at Fred's Lounge in Mamou, Louisiana

as spoons rake the washboard
drinks already flowing

the dancing wall to wall
and Tante Sue

takes the mic
and a swig from her pint of Hot Damn!

and says,
"there's only two four-letter words

that we allow in here and them's
beer and *love*!"

I've got other items like you
little mirror

just as small and cheap   scattered about
which don't have much meaning   or a story to explain them

a belt buckle   a plastic razor
socks under the bed   a dried out fountain pen

The tarnished incense Buddha on the windowsill
my grandmother lit after using the bedpan

(which I'd lay a newspaper over for her)
is no such thing

nothing *id est*
ad nauseum   or *res publica* about it

You must have a thing like that too
little mirror

that I wouldn't have the least clue about
but which explains who you are

if anything can

38

Don't you just hate it when
you don't know where the day went

and you have nothing to show for it
And who would you show it to anyway

this crystalline nothing   like iron embedded in ore
that emerged from perplexity or a hopeless feeling

Whomever you showed it to
something would get lost in translation

something you felt or thought it conveyed
would be missed or misunderstood

and the thing you conjured
that felt miraculous   as uncanny

as a coin
materialized from behind your ear

would appear unexceptional
when you pointed it out

and that person   your audience
would change the subject

and froth about some slight he'd received
or say

you'll never guess who I saw today
expecting you to be as interested

as he or she wasn't
— although   maybe it's *you*

Maybe you'd built it up in your head
all that time alone

which in the public light of day
doesn't amount to much   you now see

it was just a will-o'-the-wisp
certainly nothing to write home about

Little mirror
you have no idea what I'm talking about

do you   or how lucky you are
not to know what *pointless* or *deluded* feels like

And yet   little mirror
this story of all or nothing

may be worth the paper it's written on
Until then   it's Philippe Petit

stepping out onto a high wire at 7 a.m. of an August morning
to begin his walk between the Twin Towers a quarter mile above
          the earth

Who would have thought then
the Towers themselves would turn out to be

a house of cards

39

Little mirror
whoever propped you on the shelf

and covered you with a black cloth
has gone for good

Dust comes drifting down
mice scurry by at night

red squirrels in the eaves
release a pungent urine

Couples break in
and walk through the house

hand in hand
The little doings   the foragings

the nest making
you're taking these to the grave with you

Once you reflected back what you saw
as you saw it

Now you're a document
completely redacted

Yet somewhere there's bound to be
the original

40

A crow swoops across the mirror
like a floater in the eye

Then another flies straight into
and through it   receding

Then a murder of crows
comes flying out

like someone had raised a window
and flung out a bucket of rinse water

All day the crows keep flying
If you put your ear to the little mirror

you'll hear them
far off

gathering in the bare branches
an urgent chorus

No matter how many thousands there are
there's no safety in numbers

as the men below
raising their shotguns   will attest

41

Little mirror   lip reader
there's only so many poems
so many songs

that got their start long ago
coming toward us from a long way off
from the treetops   or the Atlas Mountains

They carry on their back
some of the older thoughts in the world:
forgiveness for what must be done

dismay at finding everyone gone
gladness at being alive against the odds
how men and women and the river itself

put eternity back into time
So few songs   at root
restless   on the move   unable

to settle down   to spread their word
All day all night   all night all day
amazing how far   how fast

they make their way
crisscrossing the green and gray world
the mineral and wet world

the vertical and cavernous world
It's hard to tell exactly when
a reverberation turns into an echo

and that echo   keeps on echoing

42

The last supper of the little mirror
has lasted

its entire lifetime
From the outset of its career

it took into itself
every plate of food that was put before it

sun cloud sleet leaf hair nose stud teeth
eyebrow earlobe tweezers uvula

That's just for starters
It never grew fat or satiated

never greedy for more   or bulimic after
never preferred one perfume over another

self-love to self-disgust   candor to vanity
tap water saliva jism toothpaste hair spray were all the same

It neither pitied nor despised anyone
It went the Buddha one better vis a vis desire

If it had another reflective cheek
it would have turned it

When the little mirror is finally betrayed
it will be only because its Judas won't know he is Judas

That's just how it goes with mirrors and wrecking balls

43

Who's to say you won't outlive
or outlast us

Uncomplaining
you'll lie in the patient earth

like stone or styrofoam
and sleep the sleep of the just

undisturbed by consciousness
And if this corn field

that was just manured the other day
is turned into a parking lot

you'll be like the remains
of Richard III

dug up in the Grey Friars
car park in Leicester

Someone will pick you out
of the dirt

and look you over a moment
before tossing you back

44

There's you   little mirror
the lake

the wide slow slithering river
and from a high bluff

the ocean
immeasurable and seething

as though I'd never seen anything
like it before

and there's you again   little mirror
unimpressive

not a force
to be reckoned with

not some hierophany of nature
I'd always dreamed of

but something
 — someone —

I could just talk to
never mind that your listening

doesn't involve hearing
that you have no empathy

You've never interrupted or grown impatient
and that's all I've needed

to tempt the hidden thing
to step out in front of the curtain

and — alone and in full view —
refuse to take a bow

45

1.

It goes without saying
               little mirror
Everything that happens
               happens at least once
A few things happen twice
               or three times
Some things happen again and again
               sometimes with variants   Sometimes
it's only the timing that's different
               like with sex or syllables   ballads or box steps
Sometimes recurrence goes without notice
               like daylight or mayonnaise or hair growth
Sometimes it's mechanical or irritating
               like someone who just won't shut up
Other times it's intolerable
               an itch you can't reach
You'd do anything to keep it from happening again
               short of murder   or not short of it

2.

A man ends up back in the hospital on life supports
               because he wouldn't go see the doctor
because he didn't want
               above all else   to be put back into the hospital
where he is now because the pain got unbearable

The lights are too bright   there's too much damn beeping
            the nurses smile at him behind surgical masks
He thinks: if *twice* were unique and *once* was repetitive
            we'd all be a lot happier
He thinks: if *often* caused wonder
            and *one-off* were tedious and predictable
if *for the very first time* felt shopworn and *love* thrived on iterations
            he'd be happy to come back from the dead
and do the do all over again

46

So many mirrors
little mirror

no dearth of them
inconspicuous as cardboard

ubiquitous as pill bugs
spread out like listening posts

wherever questions can't be asked
wherever answers can't be given

So many that
if they took up arms

they would fill the streets
chanting

in the softest of voices
take a good look around

tell me how you really feel
Or they'd say

Tell me about the day you left home
for good

Tell me what it is like to be unable
to help your sister

They would look at each of us   and
holding their gaze   we would tell them

what we'd always wished to do
to taste   to feel   to make   to make right

Little mirror   we would reveal
what we've not even told ourselves

before like dry leaves
they blow away

taking us   a piece of us
with them

47

I am putting you away now
little mirror

You have done your work
you   a thing of no account

that I found in an outhouse
pulled over by vines

Someone   before
or after   emptying his

or her bowels
picked you up and tilted you

to examine his face
or with greater effort and worry

placed it between her legs
before stepping back out

into the snow
You were sufficient

to do the trick
and now you're an artifact

of a way of life
almost unrecognizable as one

just something
to cut one's finger on

but   to me   you're a talisman
a fellow traveler

scratched   discolored   a bit of junk
still capable of reflection

yet
still able to play a part

David Weiss has published four previous collections of poems: *The Fourth Part of the World* (Ohio State University Press), *Gnomon* (Wolf at the Door Press), *Perfect Crime* (Nine Mile Books), and *Per Diem* (Tiger Bark Press) and one novel, *The Mensch*. He co-edited *The Poet's Notebook* (W.W. Norton) and his essays, translations, and poems have appeared over the years in  *The Atlantic, Parnassus, The New Yorker, Iowa Review, North American Review, Modern Poetry in Translation, Crazyhorse, Ploughshares,* and *Literary Imagination,* among others. He was editor of *Seneca Review* for many years and taught at Hobart and William Smith Colleges in Geneva, New York.